A Sistah 4CHANGE

Thoughts of a Balanced Afrikan Woman

Kimadda Agyeman

ISBN 9780615809618
ISBN 0615809618

A Sistah 4 Change
Thoughts of a Balanced Afrikan Woman
Volume 1

Edited: Bianca Bostic

Cover Illustration: Antoine Ghost Mitchell Poeartry
Creative Movement LLC
(www.poeartry.net)

Cover Design: Hot Book Covers
(www.hotbookcovers.com)

Kimadda Agyeman
Author's Foundation

Sistaz 4 Ma'at

www.sistaz4maat.com

In Loving Memory

Thelma & David Green
Mattie Bell Williams
Leonard Reed
Lamar Antonio Jenkins
Paul Antwon Wills

Dedication

To the two most important women in my life whom if it was not for you, you would not be reading this book. The woman that gave me life and the woman that reared me to be the woman I am today. I love you both and I thank you.

To my complement and best friend Sahure Nebkhau Agyeman who encouraged me to write my thoughts in a book and publish them. I am because you are.

To my two children and grandchild know that everything I do, I do it for you; this is my legacy to you.

To my siblings, nieces, and nephews I pray that you never give up on your dreams to aspire to greatness; you can be what you want to be; your destiny and power lies within you. Know Thy Self.

Acknowledgements

To the creator Odomankoma, the Abosom, and the Ancestors for framing my thoughts and guiding my pen every step of the way.

To a very special brother and lifelong friend, Avery Austin, who challenged me to look at self and to do the work that it takes to begin the process of healing by correcting those areas that caused a hindrance and stumbling block in my life. I know I kicked, screamed, and fought to get to that level of maturity in my life! I thank you for your patience and never giving up on me.

To the Akans of America my spiritual journey has ended and I have now found my home.

To my sister/brother friends in my circle who have been for there for me throughout the years in the good and bad times.

To the many Nana's, Mama's, and Baba's (Elders) who took the time to impart wisdom, knowledge, and guidance when I reached out to you; you all know who you are. Thank you.

To authors Mwalimu Baruti, Frank Edwards, Shakara Cannon, and Angela Freeman thank you for all the advice and the invaluable insight that you gave to me as a new up and coming self-published author.

To the many brothers and sisters on social media who took the time to read my random thoughts daily and to give feed back to the discussions; they were thought provoking and enlightening. To those of you who miss my daily thoughts when I take hiatuses' from social media you now have your own personal copy.

Advanced Praise

This is beautiful Queen. You are on your way to success. This is exactly what you wanted. The artwork is fabulous. I'm so happy for you; accomplishing your goals, going into the ancestral reservoir, compiling the many great thoughts you have. You are definitely "Seshat" personified. Keep up the great work. There's so much that needs to be highlighted to assist our people in their ascension. This definitely fills a major gap and gives positive and effective clarity for mending our relationships.

As you know, you cannot cater to everyone. Hopefully, the readers of this dynamic work will be able to extract from this book and find it compelling for assisting them personally and collectively. May the ancestors strengthen you, as they have been doing for so long, with this magnetic monumental endeavor.

-Sahure' Nebkhau Agyeman

I have to say that it is an easy read. You get your point across loud and clear. Whoever reads it will definitely understand what you are saying.

-Orlando Epps

Your writing voice is so smooth and easily relatable without coming across as harsh or condescending. I think that you are a great writer. I pray that everyone can receive the message from your book and know that it comes from a place of true love and hope for growth of those reading it. Keep on going girl...you are the Bomb!!!

-Bianca Bostic

Community is the spirit, the guiding light of the tribe, whereby people come together in order to fulfill a specific purpose, to help others fulfill their purpose, and to take care of one another. The goal of the community is to make sure that each member of the community is heard and is properly giving the gifts he has brought to this world.

Without this giving, the community dies. And without the community, the individual is left without a place where he can contribute. The community is that grounding place where people come and share their gifts and receive from others.

-Sobonfu Somé

Quotes

"The true worth of a race must be measured by the character of its womanhood."

-Mary McLeod Bethune

"We black men have a hard enough time in our own struggle for justice, and already have enough enemies as it is, to make the drastic mistake of attacking each other and adding more weight to an already unbearable load".

-Malcolm X

"Our purpose in life is to leave a legacy for our children and our children's children. For this reason, we must correct history that at present denies our humanity and self-respect."

-Queen Mother Moore

Author's Note

In the subtitle and throughout the book I use the term "Afrikan: instead of "African" when speaking of Black people in America (Diaspora). The reason for this is explained by author Haki R Madhubuti in his book Black Men: Obsolete, Single, Dangerous? The Afrikan American Family in Transition he explains thus:

"I used a capital "B" when referring to black people. The word Black is descriptive but it also is a political and culture term that identifies people of Afrikan descent at a world level.

In spelling Afrika I use "k" rather than "c" because for many activists the "k" represents an acknowledgment that "Africa" is not the true name of that vast continent. When I speak of Afrika, I'm bringing an Afrikan centered view to my meaning.

Therefore, the Afrika spelled with a "k" represents a redefined and potentially different Afrika, and also it symbolizes for me a coming back together of Afrikan people worldwide. Let it be understood that when I speak of Afrika and when most whites think of "Africa," we are coming from two different world views.

Table of Contents

Foreward   **4**

Preface   7

Thought Topic Chapter 1
Baby Mama/Daddy Drama   **9**

Thought Topic Chapter 2
Child Support   15

Thought Topic Chapter 3
Gender Wars   **19**

Thought Topic Chapter 4
Strong Independent Woman   25

Thought Topic Chapter 5
Healthy Relationships   **29**

Thought Topic Chapter 6
Love knows no limits   37

Thought Topic Chapter 7
Complementarity   **43**

Thought Topic Chapter 8
Fire Side Chat with our children   49

Thought Topic Chapter 9
Society Sayz   **53**

Thought Topic Chapter 10
Beauty of Sistahood   59

Closing Thoughts   **63**

Appendix A (Glossary of Terms)   65

Appendix B (Author's Contact)   **68**

Foreward
Idris Abdal Alim

The strength of A Sistah 4 Change is in its approach. Sista Kimadda Agyeman grants the reader the gift of her experiences which serve as a mirror through which we can view ourselves. In a conversational tone which is sublime, a Sista's powerful message of change is transmitted and her words resonate not only in the head, but in the heart. I have heard it said that a loving heart is the beginning of all knowledge, and I agree. Studies indicate that one person's heart signal can affect another's brainwaves, and that heart-brain synchronization can occur between two people when they interact. Kimadda Agyeman's work is that quality of personal discourse, the nature of which can serve as an adhesive for our damaged, destructive relationships. Not only is A Sistah 4 Change a touchstone for transformation, it is the result. The conversational style is also the means through which the author accesses the mind, which beautifully serves the overall purpose of her work.

For over 400 years we have lived in and under seen and unseen restraints. We were taught, told, and pressured into what to think and what to believe with

A Sistah 4 Change

no qualifiers, and no means of evaluation. We were also taught, or pressured into our behavior, how to act, and what was acceptable to Caucasians. This provided them with effective control over our minds and consequently our lives enforced by fear. Even now this environment produces various levels of trauma. Most of our people live in and out of fear, anger and confusion, unaware of the cause. The overt and the subtle indications of stress impact our capacity to interact with each other harmoniously, yet the Thoughts of a Balanced Afrikan Woman offers us hope.

Given the nature of our experiences during our sojourn here in the west, a change would require a connection with a new body of words or ideas, as it relates to who we are. A persons "self concept" produces a selective effect on his perception, if he is not conscious of his actions and or the causes of his actions. "Selective perceptions" can have either a negative or positive effect and suggests that the already existing belief about the "self" supports – whether positive or negative – those concepts that maintain and reinforce the status quo, or the "self concepts" existence. The "self concept" serves as the "glasses" or the frame of reference through and from which we make all of our observations and reach all of our conclusions. It is the personal reality from which all other things are observed and comprehended (rightly or wrongly). The "self concept" is learned as a consequence of experience, and reinforced through interaction with others, significant and generalized. As a people, the importance of the aforementioned should be clear.

5

Kimadda Agyeman

A Sistah 4 Change is Kimadda Agyeman's contribution to our 400 year old problem, it is imbued with love, the kind of love that has evolved against the most tremendous of odds. Her courage is the source of her honesty, as well as her dogged determination to exist as her innate self in a world that is not only contrary, but antagonistic. She is a Mother, and a Sister. She not only presents a new idea, she is the idea embodied, and her spirit has inspired me.

Peace

Preface

"My thoughts are my strategies; my pen and pad is how I execute"

We all have our own views and perspectives on various topics such as those mentioned throughout this book. I enjoy sharing and engaging in thought provoking topics with those in my circle, as I get to listen to other's perspectives and viewpoints. This book, comprised of various thoughts, creates an environment for readers to engage in healthy dialogue amongst family, friends, colleagues, and those in their circle.

It is my opinion, that having different perspectives allows for diversity; the world would be a pretty boring place if we all thought the same. In that respect, I do not expect everyone who reads these thoughts to agree with everything written within these pages. My views are based on my personal experiences and lifelong lessons learned, in hope that they will inspire, uplift, mend and heal the relationships and spirits of those who read it. In addition, that they become conversational pieces at the dinner table and/or in group settings as I am sure that the reader can relate in some way.

    To the readers, I want to personally thank you for taking the journey into the mentality of a Balanced Afrikan Woman whose mission in life is to heal, restore, inspire, educate, encourage, empower, and enrich the lives of the people whom she encounters in her life daily.

Peace & Blessings
Kimadda Agyeman

Thought Topic Chapter 1
Baby Mama/Daddy Drama

"When you bear a grudge, your child will also bear a grudge."
Rwandese Proverb

Where do I begin? There is so much that I could say about this topic. I used to be of the mindset that only young teenage sisters and brothers that have children experience this drama. It was not until I had to experience it myself in my early forties, that I realized that baby mama/daddy drama is not defined by age; however, it is indeed defined by ones maturity level.

Why is it that when a brother or sister whom you had a child with one day decide for whatever reason to end the relationship and move on with their life that it is hard for the child's mother or father to move on with their lives? Often time it happens more with the sisters than the brothers being that the child usually stays with the mother the majority of their life.

Kimadda Agyeman

During the whole time that the brother or sister is single and not in a committed relationship with anyone the baby mama/daddy is cool, no drama at all; the child gets to spend time with their mother or father on a regular basis. However, when they do meet someone and decide to begin a relationship with them and the baby mama/daddy finds out that is when the drama begins.

Case in point Jay and Stacy, fictional names, meet through mutual friends. They exchange numbers and begin to go out on dates, during the course of getting to know one another they realize that they have a lot in common and enjoy each other's company. After dating for a while they decide to make it official and be exclusive to one another. They both have daughters from previous relationships; and a history of being good parents to their children.

Jay and Stacey decide that it is time for them to meet each other's children. Stacey's daughter's father is not active in her life, so she does not see him as such there is no baby daddy drama for Jay to encounter. Stacey on the other hand does. Jay calls his baby mama Sasha to let her know that he is on his way to come pick up their daughter and that he will be bringing his new lady with him. Oh boy, now the fireworks begin. Sasha tells him that she does not want his new lady around their daughter; mind you Stacey has no history of child abuse or neglect and even in that Jay's baby mama does not want their daughter around her. I wonder why? I'll tell you why; because as long as Jay was single, and with no other woman, Sasha was fine, however, now that he

A Sistah 4 Change

is happy and in a full filling relationship his baby mama is upset because deep down inside she still has feelings for him even though he has made it very clear that he no longer feels the same way about her. Jay still wants to be in his daughter life. What an upstanding Black man. Jay tells Stacey what transpired between him and Sasha and although Stacey is apprehensive and does not care to deal with the baby mama drama because of her love and commitment to Jay and the acceptance of his daughter she attempts to reach out to Sasha and establish a relationship with her. Sasha insists on not having any dealings with Stacey. Stacey still decides to stay in the relationship with Jay because she knows that he is a good man. What a great Black woman.

One day Jay and Stacey decide to take their two children out to the park for family time however, Jay's daughter is not there. Sasha will not let Jay see their daughter because he is in a relationship with Stacey. This takes an emotional toll on Jay and affects him deeply; he is used to seeing and spending time with his daughter, and now he has not seen her in a while; all because Sasha refuses to accept the fact that he has moved on with his life. This is one story and I know of many other's including mine.

A message to the baby mama

Sister if this is you that I described in the aforementioned case then you really need to take a long hard look at yourself. When you refuse to allow the father of your child to see his daughter/son you are not

11

hurting the father you are hurting the child. Moreover, if you are the reason that the brother left in the first place, because of the things you did or did not do then that is no one's fault but your own. Why does the child have to suffer and not be allowed to see their father if that is what they want? I mean you tell your child negative things about their dad, that may not even be true, which in turn causes the child to begin to hate and despise their father. When you do that it comes back to bite you in your ass, because once the child grows older and learns the real truth about their father and the lies you told to keep them from him they will resent you and they will not want to have any dealings with you; once again it will be no one's fault but your own. Think about it; is that how you want your child to view you as their mother?

Sister if you are the reason that the brother left as I mentioned before you need to take a self-examination and find out where you went wrong and work to fix those issues so that they will not continue in your next relationship. A lot of times we do not want to look in the mirror because we are afraid of what we may see; it is easier for us to take the focus off of self and point the finger at the brotha. What is even sadder is that if and when the brother does want to see his child he has to jump through hoops to cater to you in order to see his own child because you are emotionally unstable and not thinking logically about the ramifications that I mentioned earlier about the child resenting you. I am not making excuses for the brothers that refuse to put up with the drama and stop seeing their children; however,

A Sistah 4 Change

it is what it is. Sister as a mother all that was spoken above is not worth it. Let the child/ren see their father even if he does not want to be in a relationship with you. Grow up, Get over it and move on because there is nothing more tragic than a child to hate the womb that he/she came from; the woman that gave them life.

A message to the baby daddy

Brother if you have a child by a woman and you two are no longer together and she has moved on with her life; however, she still wants you to be in your child's life; don't come around the new man starting trouble with him and talking about another brother is not going to rear your son/daughter. The same applies to you in the case of Jay and Sasha, if the brother is of good character and has no history of child abuse/neglect or what have you, then there should be no issues. I am not sure what it is about the man that causes him to think like that as I am not a man unless like the sisters he still has feelings for his baby mama. However, I will say this, that if the man is mature than I am sure that he will sit down with you and let you know that he is not there to replace you as the child's father and there is nothing that you should be threatened by with him being in your child's life. It is important for the sake of the child that you too establish a relationship with the new man so that you all can live in peace with a harmonious life.

Thought Topic Chapter 2
Child Support

"Children are the reward of life"
Afrikan Proverb

I will begin by saying that if a brother has intimate relations with a sister and she gives birth to a child then it is both parents responsibility to provide for the needs of that child mentally, emotionally, physically, and financially. Now that I got that out of the way this message speaks to the countless number of Black brothers in our community who are in the child support system. I know of a couple of good brothers who are very close to me, whose lives have been damaged because of scorned women who diabolically and deliberately set out to destroy our Black men.

I am not an advocate for putting a brother in the system and I will explain why later. My position in terms of child support is that if the father of the child is willing to work with the mother and assist her in rearing their child/ren as well as giving something financial towards them then why would a mother take the father to court. Moreover, if the father no longer wants to be involved with the mother than my position is move on sister and do what is best for the child/ren. I get irate with sisters that will deliberately not allow the father to see his child/ren because he is no longer married or in a relationship with her; I elaborated on this in the topic of baby mama/daddy drama, there is more to rearing and supporting a child then money.

Speaking from experience the fathers of my two children were not active or a part of their lives for whatever reason. I can honestly say that it was nothing on my part, I can assure you of that. Although, it hurt me that they did not become a part of their lives, I did not go out and file for child support. I cannot speak to everyone's circumstances; however, for me I was gainfully employed at the time and was making enough money to provide for my children. My position was I would rather have their father's spend time with them, instead of giving me money if they did not have it to give. Giving money is easy; however, spending quality time with them is even better.

Now to the father of the child/ren who just out right refuse to support the child financially or any other way; that is a different story and he should be ashamed of himself. Especially if he is gainfully employed and does not come around and spend quality time with their child/ren. Although, I am not an advocate for going through the court system to get support for a child I do not condone or accept the irresponsibility of the father for not providing for his child.

As I stated above, I am not an advocate for going through the corrupt court system for child support because it damages men on so many different levels and once they are in the system it is hard to have any normalcy in their lives.

I have been told stories by brothers of passports and driver's licenses being revoked, they cannot leave out the country or drive. Now if that is the case then I am trying to understand what if a brother's license is suspended how can he go and look for a job to support his child/ren if he cannot drive? What if the location of the job that is hiring is not accessible through public transportation? Moreover, what if there is a job opening for a licensed driver the brother still cannot apply for the position because of the issue with his license. It's like a catch twenty two. You damned if you do and damned if you don't.

In terms of the woman scorned, we all have been hurt in our lives from previous relationships, I know that I have on many occasions; however, I would never set out to deliberately destroy someone's character be it a brother or sister. That is not cool at all. To address the sisters who set out to do this to the father of your child, is just dead wrong and it speaks volume of their character; they should be ashamed of themselves. What does it do for them to destroy someone's credibility and refuse to allow him to see his child/ren? I know for a fact that some not all hurt people hurt other people.

Kimadda Agyeman

One final thought on this topic and that is there is becoming a lot of single fathers in our community who have custody of their child/ren. My position on this still remains the same for the woman as I spoke about the man. Sister if you are not taking responsibility for the rearing of your child/ren physically, financially or emotionally then that is not a good thing. Sister's we are the givers of life which is the most beautiful thing that the creator has given us the ability to do; to bear children and once they come here on this physical plane it is the man and the woman's responsibility to see that the child is reared in a loving and stable home. I just hope for the sake of the child/ren that the man and woman can work out some type of an amicable agreement where either one of their lives are not ruined because of the corrupt court system.

Thought Topic Chapter 3
Gender Wars

*"We can't have war between black women and men,
because no people can be free if one half of the mind
of the people is tied up in conflict. It's going to have to
be both of us or none of us"*
Dr. John Henrik Clarke

I am not an avid television watcher as I do a lot of
reading, writing, and research so most of my time
outside of work and family is spent reading, journalizing
or browsing the web, so my television for the majority
of the time when I am home is off. Ok so, I was sitting
at home relaxing on the sofa one evening and just to
break up the monotony a bit I decided to see what was
on television. I first tuned in on the news and that was
depressing, plus the media cannot be trusted as most of
it is propaganda that is another reason why it stays off.

Since the news was so depressing I just continued
to surf the channels to see what else was on, I like to
look at documentaries and educational programs. As an
air sign a Gemini I have a constant need to be mentally

stimulated as long as it is purposeful and productive. I digress a bit. As I proceeded to flip through the channels I saw a television show called "Love and Hip Hop" and I have heard that there are others. I have not sought to look at them after what I saw this night. Ok, so as I was looking at the show a part came on where this sister was giving this brother a serious tongue lashing, I mean she tore that brother down so bad that I am surprised that he was still able to walk away with his manhood intact. Then in another scene the brother is tearing the sister down and then finally two of the sister's scream and fight at one another. I mean they were going at it so much that I had to rise up and sit on the edge of the sofa while shaking my head in dismay.

I know that this was television and that television is used as a tool to program the minds of the people; I mean they don't call it programming for nothing it has a purpose and to make matters worse it is coined a reality show; which entails being real. Our sisters and brothers, and even our children, tune into reality television shows like these weekly and then get drawn into them to the point that they begin to live out the behaviors depicted in the reality show in their own lives. To the unsuspecting viewer believes that this stuff really goes on in the lives of the people playing these roles, in actuality they don't even live and act like this in reality. These shows are scripted; these are actors/actresses. It is not real!

Shows of this kind promote the derogatory stereotypes of how people view the Black man and woman as it pertains to relationships and family. Our

A Sistah 4 Change

people are constantly bombarded with negative images and behaviors depicted in these reality television programs which shows a moral decline in the structure of the Black family. Moreover, these shows have set us back on so many different levels as Black people.

My sisters and brothers we cannot continue to partake in the madness that these reality shows depict, despite how entertaining they may seem. When we sit down at the television and watch shows like these it builds up the ratings of the channel and the more the ratings go up the more they will continue to keep shows like this in syndication. When we sit and watch we add fuel to their power. I am speaking of those who are in control of the media and television programming that keeps us dumbed down and shows us how dysfunctional we are. We have to wake up my people.

I know that there is no perfect man or woman and yes, we all have some sort of dysfunction in our families and yes, get into arguments and/or disagreements with one another that is a reality. However, we have to work towards rebuilding our relationships between the Black man and woman. We have to stop pointing the finger at one another and playing the blame game. We have to stop tearing one another down because our children are dying in the streets; they are being locked up and all sorts of other things. When we brothers and sisters are at each other's throats we in turn loose our children. What kind of example are we being to them when we act like this? If the Black man and woman is at war then our children will be at war. We have to build one another up,

21

not tear each other down. We are a loving, caring and compassionate people. When we brothers and sisters display this madness that we see on television in our own personal lives this is nothing more than the results of Mentacide.

My foundation Sistaz 4 Ma'at emphasizes a firm conviction that in spite of the current condition and state of the Black family, with the Rites of passage project that we provide the relationship between the Black man and woman can be mended, healed and restored to bring the Black family back to its greatness; where we showed love and respect to one another; where we took the time to come together at family gatherings and reunions as well as played a role in not only our own children lives, but in the lives of other families children as well.

A Sistah 4 Change

To be An Afrikan Woman

Afrikan women told the stories and passed on the culture in their breast milk. We held our men and let them cry and we cried in the strength of their arms. To Be An Afrikan Woman is to know that we, Afrikan men and women, are the mirrors of each other's souls in which we find our ability to love, and to be loved. To Be An Afrikan Woman is to know that your man is the voice which affirms your womaness. It is to be able to feel him say "You are an Afrikan Woman". To Be An Afrikan Woman is to be the Memory of the race, which makes Sankofa possible. It is to "bury the placenta" so that Afrika can be resurrected. To Be An Afrikan Woman is to pick up the pieces of our Maafa-shattered lives and to make our people whole again. It is to Rebirth the Spirit of Afrika.
    -Dr. Marimba Ani

Thought Topic Chapter 4
The Strong Black Independent Woman

A strong black woman is not a woman who is independent and says that she don't need a man; a strong black woman is a woman who has been through trials and tribulations and still came through with love, beauty and character

Kimadda Agyeman

Sisters I know there are a lot of us out here who are gainfully employed, have our own homes, cars and money and we feel or say that we don't need a man for anything because we can hold our own. That much is true in terms of not needing him to pay or help pay for those material possessions; however, I myself do need a man in my life. I need a man to be intimate with, to share my life with; a man who can be a protector for me. I enjoy the company of a Black man for mental stimulation and balance. I love the way the Black man smells; the way he walks; the way he talks; the way he looks; the way he smiles. I love his thick lips and broad nose; the way he dresses; his stature; his strength and the feel of his hands caressing my body while lying in his arms and talking until we fall asleep. What a beautiful thing! Whoa child, I had to stop writing and take a deep breath.

Aight, Kimadda get yourself together girl and bring it back in. I tell you; I love me some Black men. Angie Stone has a song titled "Brotha" and I just love to listen to that song and watch that video. I even share that video with the brotha's on social media who I love and respect. It is a testament to who and what the Black man is to his family and community. Sisters the Black man needs you just like we need them; we need each other. We need balance and structure in our community.

Well to get back to the thought at hand, being a strong black independent woman in my thought paradigm does not exist. Allow me to explain; the word independent entails not relying on another or others for aid or support. There is a saying that no man is an island, as you know an island sits off in the water by itself; every one of us in the world need someone for one thing or another so we must be realistic about this. Moreover, who in their right state of mind wants to be all alone and to themselves all of the time? I know that I do not, and I am sure that others who are reading this feel the same way.

The quote spoken by Dr. Marimba Ani on the preceding page spoke volumes and I had to share it with the readers as it is a precursor to who and what we were before this whole "I am a strong black independent woman and I don't need a man" thing came about. According to the Afrikan world view Black men and

A Sistah 4 Change

women were and still are interdependent, which entails being mutually dependent or depending on each other; we needed that as we Afrikans are a communal people. I cannot stress that enough.

Many sisters such as myself have been through so much in our lives whether the situation was brought on by ourselves or from the actions of others. Depending on the situation and the person some of us come through and some of us don't. Those of us that do make it through the storms of life may become angry or bitter as a result of that situation, and then there are some of us who try to come to the resolve of what happened and look to put mechanisms in place so that it will not become a reoccurring situation. I have had people that have violated and abused me and I had a right to be angry. However, I refuse to walk around as the stereotypical angry, Black scorned and damaged woman. I had to work to let that stuff other's had di to me go, and forgive them as well as forgive myself for the things I brought on myself, for my own sanity.

I am not going to walk around and let people who violated me still have power over me by harboring what they did to me. They have moved on with their life and I chose to move on with mine; to live a happy, peaceful and carefree life. There is a saying that whatever does not kill you makes you stronger. I say this not to boast; however, humbly. I came through my trials and tribulations and I still project a spirit of love and beauty; those who know me personally can attest to that. Sisters let's strive daily at becoming an Interdependent woman and not an Independent woman.

27

Thought Topic Chapter 5
Healthy Relationships

"Some of the biggest challenges in relationships come from the fact that most people enter a relationship in order to get something: they're trying to find someone who's going to make them feel good. In reality, the only way a relationship will last is if you see your relationship as a place that you go to give and not a place that you go to take".

Anthony Robbins

I know that this is a very broad topic and the aforementioned quote can be plugged into any relationship be it mother/daughter/father/son/ siblings/distance relatives/sister friends or brother friends; however, I would like to talk about the relationship between a man and a woman. Now I am no relationship specialist per se; however, I have been in enough and have gained a lot of wisdom and understanding and learned a lot of lessons over the years from being in a few, three to be exact, including this one. The longest was 10 years. In my experience with searching for love or that perfect mate, which there is no such thing as a perfect mate, and I will expound on that a little bit later. I have found that a lot of times we go into relationships looking for someone to fill the voids that we have in our life unbeknownst to the man/woman you are with. Then when they do not fill those voids we become disillusioned or disappointed and we end the relationship with them only to move on to the next one, still empty and looking, until it becomes a never ending cycle which only leads to more heart ache and pain. Ask me how I know? Been there, done that.

I would like to take a minute to have a heart to heart with my sisters. Most of the conversations and the things we speak about are men and the failure with finding a suitable mate. What I have found to be a pattern with most sisters is we have a habit of letting the brothers dig into the treasure chest and take what they want too soon without getting to know the brother and when the brother gets what he wants then he is off and moving on to the next sister; please know that I am not speaking and lumping all brothers into one bag I am just speaking about the ones that do.

I know that a lot of times we sisters are insecure and have low self-esteem; we feel the need to be validated by others. There are brothers who know and prey on the psyche of the sisters that are in that state of mind; they should be ashamed of themselves. Brothers if you know that a sister is in that state and you only seek to turn her out and make her feel less about herself, then you are wrong and have violated the womb that you came

A Sistah 4 Change

out. Sisters, if you see a brother and he is handsome and single, because you are lonely and want some intimacy he may say a few smooth words and compliments with his mack game, don't immediately fall for that. Moreover, sisters be mindful of how you engage in a conversation with a brother because a lot of times we sisters say words that leads the brother on, and when that happens he monopolizes on that then proceeds to come onto you even more and when that happens we sisters become all moist and heated in between our thighs and then we are ready to spread open our legs and allow the brothers to enter into heaven only to find out later that he desecrated it and moved on to the next sister. Sisters you just cannot point the blame at the brothers you are also to blame as you allowed this to happen.

My sisters and brothers we must get to know a person's mind/spirit instead of just falling in love with the thought of having someone. Moreover, we sisters need to keep our legs closed and our emotions in check until we know for sure that the brother is sincere in his desire to seek a complement. I know this may be a challenge for some of us sisters; however, trust me I know from experience that you can do it. I did it for two years. I did not date nor speak with any brothers on an intimate personal level. In addition I remained celibate and just worked on myself (mind, body and spirit). I mean I treated our brothers like they had the plague in terms of trying to seek out and establish a relationship with them; therefore, it was easier just not to even entertain the thought of having a man. Did that stop the brothers from trying to get to know me? No it did

Kimadda Agyeman

not, they would still come on to me and I was just like no I'm cool, or I am not interested. I mean I was just tired of the heartache and pain that comes with trying to love a man; a Black broken man at that; because we as a people have suffered and endured so much since we were brought to these shores against our will and with going through the Maafa or Middle passage, which ever you choose to call it, damaged us mentally and we are still trying to regain our sanity our Afrikan state of mind that we had before the Maafa. It was not until I took a hiatus from brothers and wanting, needing and desiring to be in a relationship that I met my complement.

Now back to my sisters and brothers who say that they are waiting on the perfect man/woman; some even take it as far as to say that they are waiting on Jesus to bring them their mate. I used to be of that mind state when I was in the religion of Christianity; I have since left and suffice to say that during the time I was there and waiting on Jesus to send me my mate he never came. Jesus did not deliver and that is not the reason that I left. That is a whole different topic for another time. Oh well, as I mentioned above; I myself took the time to use my brain and mental faculties that I was born with to choose my complement after taking the time to work on self. We as a people have been taught and conditioned to look without instead of within. When you go within, that is when you get the answers and the things that you want, need and desire.

Speaking of the perfect man or woman; to be perfect entails to be entirely without flaws, defects,

A Sistah 4 Change

or shortcomings; now let's be real here we know that as humans that is impossible. Those of us who are in search of a complement have to be realistic about that. That kind of mentality is of the extreme; on the flip side of that you have some sisters who say that well I rather have a piece of a man than no man at all; or they say well he got some shit with him; however, that's my piece of a man; this too is of the extreme.

My sisters and brothers we must find a balance when we are in pursuit of a complement or are currently in one that is barely hanging by a thread. Why would a sister want a piece of a man rather than a whole man? A whole man is a man who is cognizant of his flaws and shortcomings; yet he is putting forth the effort to correct those areas in his life. Whereas a piece of a man could really care less about that; he's just going to do him, with a mentality like that it only leads to collateral damage.

How many of you reading this book remember the late 1960's early 70's television comedy sit com about romance titled "Love American Style"? Well for those of you who do or don't know the sitcoms theme song has a chorus that says "Love American style that's me and you". Well here is my version and trust me, mine was not a comedy; it was a drama. This is how I love, so take notes. I wrote this poem to my ex when we were going through some real trying times in our relationship. We eventually parted ways.

33

Kimadda Agyeman

"Love Kimadda Style"

Musiq sayz love so many people use your name in vain; love those who have faith in you sometimes go astray; through all the ups and down the joy and hurt for better or worse I still choose you first. How true I find these lyrics to be people say that word so loosely can't you see.

It never cease to amaze me how we tell that special someone we love them each and every day but when shit hit's the fan or things don't go our way we turn and walk away.

If true and unconditional love is divine my love for you has stood the test of time

Love Kimadda style that's me and you

Why people use the word love in vain I will never know then again I retract that statement cuz love is an action we must show so in reality I do know why we use it in vain cuz we are so shallow and superficial and use it for selfish gain.

You told me so many times that you love me not only in English as well as Spanish the last time we spoke those words vanished
Again we spoke and I longed to hear those words reappear cuz they were like a sweet melody to my ears not only that you seem far rather than near.

A Sistah 4 Change

Oh how I missed all those things you said to me and I
know they were true to a certain degree I say to a certain
degree cuz if we don't manifest love in our actions then
it becomes vain do you agree

If true and unconditional love is divine my love for
you has stood the test of time.

Love Kimadda style that's me and you.

Even though our love is going through some trying
times right now I must remain strong for the both of us
so I'mma keep holding it down

I know our spirits were intertwined by a divine source
that is why I know that our love has not run its course

So many people have said Kimadda let him go just
chalk it up as a lesson learned and move on with your
life cuz God has someone better

I understand they mean well I have to break it down
and let them know the heart of the matter

True love is deeper than a lesson learned I have
invested so much I be damned if I'mma loose out on
my return

I won't move on I choose to stick around and stand
my ground crazy it sounds I can do that cuz my emotions
are stable and not on a merry go round
See dat's what I'm saying how people just throw it

Kimadda Agyeman

all away so easy is beyond me, whatever their reason are
for giving up so easy is on them however when you love
Kimadda style it's unconditional cuz it has no beginning
or end.

If true and unconditional love is divine my love for
you have stood the test of time

Love Kimadda style that's me and you

I'mma say this one last thing then I'm through with
this piece not with you I am a firm believer that true and
unconditional love bear all things, believe all things,
hope all things, endure all things

So as long as I stay true to me I will continue to stand
on our love I will not be moved cuz I know without a
shadow of a doubt this was meant to be understood.

If true and unconditional love is divine my love for
you have stood the test of time

Love Kimadda style that's me and you.

Thought Topic Chapter 6
Love Knows no Limit

Love has to be shown by deeds not words.
Swahili proverb

*I*magine this! You meet a very tall, handsome brother who is a little rough around the edges. You know the type who has a little street in him. In the beginning he seems real cool; you both feel a good vibe with one another so exchange numbers and you spend long hours at night talking on the phone on just about any and everything you can think of; I mean as an adult you feel like a teenager again; Yeah you know what I mean; both of you are tired but you don't want to get off the phone; eventually one of you decide to just say good night and hang up. The next day you get up; you may call or text just to say good morning or was sup baby just checking on you and vice versa; you see his/her call and then a big smile comes upon your face and you sit there grinning like a Cheshire cat.

Well the two of you decide to go out and have dinner/movies or whatever and you have such a good

Kimadda Agyeman

time with each other that after dating for a while you decide that you will be exclusive to one another (or at least I said that I would). If I could pause here for a moment I just like to say that when I am in a committed relationship with a brother it is all about him; no other brother matters to me; I don't even look at another brother with inappropriate looks as I have tunnel vision when it comes to my man. In my two past relationships, and my current one, I never cheated or stepped outside of my union. I was and am committed and faithful.

Ok so back to what I was saying; so you both are kicking it and eventually as time progresses you become sexually intimate with one another; you exchange energies which that within itself is a whole other topic; maybe I will speak more about it in another volume. The love making is so good and you just get hooked; or what they now call "Dickmatized" or "Booty whipped" and after that happens all your, well most of your logical senses, go out the window and you start subjecting yourself to all kinds of bull shit just to have a man or a woman or good sex. Wait a minute! Hold up! I am jumping ahead of myself. Well, I am sure that you know where all of this is going, so I will not write a script for you as I am sure that you can relate to what I am saying. Which brings me to this, more often than not it is us sisters in the relationship because of how we are designed emotionally after you find out that the brothers has been lying, cheating and stealing from you that it affects us deeply to our core because some of us sisters such as myself love real hard; and when we love like that there is no holding back; we give our all even to the

A Sistah 4 Change

point of losing ourselves in the man that we begin to go down in our looks as well as our health; we Black sisters tend to love our Black men with all of our heart, mind, body and soul. I know of some sisters who have gone to jail because of a man and all sorts of things that they put up with because the sex was so damn good; we lose sight and focus on what is most important to us and that is ourselves.

Don't get me wrong, I can sympathize with my brothers as well who experience these things. I love my sisters, I have to admit that some of us can be a piece of work and we are just as scandalous as some of the brothers even to the point that we begin to think and act like them.

My sister, my brother I have been through so much in my last two relationships that after the second one happened. I just had to take a hiatus from getting involved with any other brother. I mean, I let these men come into my home; they had keys to my home, so they could come and go anytime. I brought them material possessions and even gave them money when they did not have it. This is just me; this is who I am and I make any apologies for that. These brothers did not use me because the things I gave them I wanted them to have. I am wired this way, and at this juncture in my life and at my age I am pretty much set in my ways so that will never change. However, I have grown and matured since these last two relationships and I have learned how to protect my heart/spirit while at the same time still not hold back love for my complement.

Kimadda Agyeman

I just have a few more things to say before I end this thought. Have you ever been so much in love that when they hurt you it feels like your heart/spirit is being torn in two? That is a feeling that I never hope to experience again. The poem that preceded this page is a result of that last relationship. I mean I have to give the brother credit if he is reading this he knows who he is. What I went through with him was the most crucial pain that I have ever felt, I had to go within myself and really search and dig deep to find out why I attracted this man and the previous one into my life and yielded the same results. I have always had a love for the underdog. I probably should not have used that word because when a man cheats he is considered a dog. When I speak of a brother in that respect I am talking the blue collar brother, the brother who may have had a record or been to jail in the past; the brother who has to get around town by public transportation or live in the hood you know the brother may not have much material wise; however, I would still love him and accept him for who he is regardless to what he has or does not have.

Final thought, I know that sometimes we become inpatient because of our need, want and desire to love and to be loved it is nothing wrong with that. We should look to seek that as human beings with emotions. However, we must learn to think critically when it comes to choosing our mate and make sure, before we choose that we know and are aware of our strengths, weaknesses, insecurities and vulnerabilities. We have to be in-tuned with ourselves in Mind, Body and Spirit because moving too quickly and in haste can cloud our

40

A Sistah 4 Change

judgment and then we end up choosing someone that can be detrimental to our health and well-being. Trust me I know been there done that and I refuse to live like that again.

Kimadda Agyeman

"Afrikan love is pure, reaffirming, assuring, self defining, balanced, wholesome, and self validating."

I would never jeopardize our union. Our asili will remain locked and our nucleus will be the most sacred inner sanctuary of protection. Our spirits mesh and unify and revive ancient souls who have struggled for us to meet again

Sahure '

Just sitting here imagining what my life would be like without you;
Out of all the Afrikan warrior women in the world you chose me to unite to;
Under no circumstances will I ever take your love for granted;
Rest assure that my love for you will never grow scanted;
Nothing in this world will ever separate us two; I vowed to protect our love and give my life for you;
Each and every day I never think twice about choosing you as my consort;
You have expressed to me in words and deeds Ma'at and that we will not abort.
      -Kimadda

Topic Thought Chapter 7
Complementarity

"A woman is a flower in a garden; her husband is the fence around it"
African Proverb

There he was with a profile picture displaying his red/black/green head band with his ankh in his hand. The site was Afraka.com. A site owned by an Afrikan brotha that is dedicated to our ancestors and reserved for other Afrikans who want to learn and gain knowledge of self, our story and our culture.

There on the site members can post videos, articles, have a live web cam, chat and post threads with topics as it relates to the Afrikan experience here in the Diaspora and on the continent. This is just one of many Afrikan owned sites where Sahure and I were members. While communicating with Sahure on line at the various socials sites we both recognized that we had a lot in common on various levels. We both had the same visions and goals as it pertained to our growth in knowledge,

Kimadda Agyeman

wisdom and understanding of our own need to work towards re-Afrikinization (Sankofa) as individuals and the collective with our people.

What attracted me to Sahure was his undying love, loyalty and commitment towards Afrika and the re-Afrikinization of our people and his beautiful Spirit. When we communicated online or saw each other online we shared knowledge and information about our story; we had long discussions about Afrika, the condition and state of our people and our liberation. At the onset of our connection we were drawn to each other's intelligence. Sahure has a beautiful mind. Funny thing is when we first met there was no attraction there in terms of being lustful or wanting to hook up with him as anything more than just friends and he felt the same way about me; Sahure never came onto to me in an inappropriate manner he was always on the real. He, like myself, was and still is a cool down to earth brother who loves to socialize and meet new, fun and interesting people. We both were genuine. The more we began to talk and get to know one another the more we realized that we were complementarity to one another on many different levels.

I can remember the times when we were online and we both were on threads dropping science and he and I would tag team a lot of people! What I mean is that our thoughts and views as it pertained to the posts being discussed where in sync with one another, that we would shut those threads down with the knowledge that we put out there. The brother was sharp and so was I. We were

A Sistah 4 Change

the Bonnie and Clyde for Afrikan Liberation. That was my comrade on the battlefield; my revolutionary warrior brother and I was his revolutionary warrior sister; we just meshed.

I would like to point out; that the most beautiful thing that I can say about our union is that online it is very hard to get to know someone on a more deep and personal level. I mean it is the internet where people create and live out lives that are not necessarily true.

How do you know if the profile picture that someone has up is really them? The only way you can get to know if the picture is them is if you use a webcam and even that is still not enough to get to know them online. Therefore, when we met in person he was the same Sahure that he was online and I was the same person. The rest well as they say is history.

Well, that's all the details; we have to keep some of our life out of the public eye. I just wanted to share our story to encourage others who are seeking a complement to never give up on love and finding your complement, they are out there. It just has to be at the opportune time. I must say that wherever you are or whatever you are doing in your life usually your complement is right there; the thing is do you recognize them and they you?

There are still a lot of good sisters and brothers out there. The thing is we miss out on them because of what they have or may not have or even what they look like or what they don't look like. A lot of times when we

45

do meet someone the first thing we look for is material possessions. What kind of car they drives, house they live in and clothes they wear and finally where do they work and what kind of work do they do. All of these things play a factor when seeking a complement; what gets me is that; we ask what you have to offer or bring to the table and that is a good question to ask and what we look for is the material possessions; my position is what if he/she does not have the latest and greatest does that mean that they can no longer be considered a suitable mate. Moreover, what if they have character interms of bringing love, loyalty, honesty, trust, and commitment to the table; is that not sufficient enough? They may not be in a position to acquire those things or they do not see the need to waste their money on material possessions. I would rather choose a brotha who possesses the aforementioned character traits over material possessions. Why? Because when you possess those traits they last if that is what your union was established on and it is your foundation. Having good quality character traits is what keeps a union together not material possessions. When the material is gone; the love and such is still there.

Sahure and I have been in a union for a year now. We have been through a lot within that year from outsiders trying to destroy our nucleus, which did not happen because it was locked and protected by the ancestors; however, instead of it tearing us apart it made us stronger and brought us closer together. What we strive to do in our union is ensure that we ourselves do not work to tear it apart; so far we have done good.

A Sistah 4 Change

I love the fact that we are still together, rising in love and growing strong while still getting to know one another. We both have been in some bad relationships where all the love that we gave was not reciprocated. That has now changed for us. I was so tired of being in one sided relationships where I was doing all the giving and now I can finally say that I know and feel what it is to give love and to have that love reciprocated; it is a beautiful feeling and for that I give thanks.

One final thought, just because you are complementarity in most areas does not mean that you will be complementarity in every area. There will be times that you may not agree with each other or have different thought paradigms and that is not such a bad thing. Since I have been on this planet I have never known anyone to have the same exact thought paradigm on every level as another. If there is then please I want to meet them.

Thought Topic Chapter 8
Fire side chat with our children

A child is what you put into him.
Nigerian Proverb

As a young mother I did not always sit down and have talks with my oldest child; even six years later after giving birth to my second child at the age of 24 I still did not have a whole lot of sit down with my children. It was not until they were close to being in their early teens that I began to really sit down and have fire side chats, is what I call them, with them.

I was a single mom rearing two children and working a full time job, so by the time I would get home check homework, cook dinner and prepare for the next day I was tired. When I got them off to bed which was about 9:00pm, at the latest I would shower and go to bed.

Our children have so much to contend with in this 21st century they are bombarded with so many negative images and music that is derogatory and degrading; peer

Kimadda Agyeman

pressure; teen pregnancy; drugs and gangs. I wish and I am sure that some of you who have young children could just keep them locked up forever in the home to protect them from the environment that they are subjected to in the streets. This method as we know is not realistic nor is it obtainable; with that being said we as parents have to take the time out to sit down and build a rapport with our children as much as possible. I know that when we sit down and speak with them they tend to retain some of it, maybe not all.

As I sit and reflect on the aforementioned proverb while writing, it reminds me that as a mother it is innate in us to love, nurture, guide and instill in them principles, as it pertains to moral and ethical character while they are still young. In my view I did the best that I could, with what I knew at the time, to instill those things in them so that they would not make some of the mistakes I made when I was young. I mean, I think back to when I was a little girl and growing up in the hood we were subject to some things; however, it was not like it is now. Which is even the more reason why we have to carve some time out in our lives to talk with our children. When we don't take the time out to do this then we do not know what our children are dealing with in their lives. I know sometimes they want to share and sometimes they don't. However, we must leave the lines of communication open with our children, so that they feel that they can come and talk to us about anything, even though we know that they don't always tell us everything, but what they want us to know.

50

A Sistah 4 Change

I know for me having to work and be out of the home for several hours of the day my children were latch key children. Those of you who do not know what a latch key child is, it is a child who has a key to their home and when they got out of school they go straight to the house and wait until the parent got home before they could go outside. They were not allowed to turn on the stove and cook so I had food for them to make sandwiches and a snack for when they got home, that was fine until I could get home to cook. Also, they were not allowed to turn the television on until they were finished with their homework.

When I did get home I let them go out for a little while and play and then once dinner was ready they came in washed up and sat at the table to eat. During the time that we were at the dinner table I would have the television set off and we would spend this time talking and sharing how our day went. This was also an opportune time for me to instill some things into them for their own good. I would like to pause and digress for a moment; what I just described that took place in my home was something that I learned to do on my own through trial and error because growing up in my home we did not do that and it was ok because I still turned out very well. I am successful; I have achieved and accomplished much in my life despite some of the obstacles and challenges that I had to endure during my late teens.

My two children are adults now and although I did take the time to sit down and have fire side chats with them as I began to mature as a woman and a mother I can say that although they did not follow everything that I spoke to them about. They have made a few choices that I am not proud of. I would have to say that I did pretty well.

My final thought to the parents who children have gone astray and/or are wayward; although you did the best that you could with what you had and knew at the time of them growing up to prevent them from making those choices. There is a Afrikan proverb that says" Parents give birth to the body of their children, but not always to their characters." Our Ancestor's on the continent of Afrika had so much wisdom and they have passed that down to us, from generation to generation. Just know that as long as you know with everything in you that you did what you did to the best of your ability and they went astray anyhow it is not your fault, the choices that we make in our lives whether good or bad will always have a consequence to it and we who make those choices be it an adult or a child have to live with that. It is universal law and as most know, the Universe does not discriminate.

Thought Topic Chapter 9
Society Says

"Knowledge without wisdom is like water in the sand"
   African proverb

Maturity at Age 18!

   Those of us who have a child/children (biological or not); we rear them and do the best that we can as a parent, be it if we are a single parent doing it by ourselves or we have the child/children's mother or father assisting us with their rearing. Society states that at the age of 18 years they are considered legal adults. Dictionary.com defines adult:

   Adult - having attained full size and strength; grown up; mature, adult person, animal, or plant.

   In my own life and assessment of being an adult, I have learned that it comes with a lot of responsibility. Being an adult means having to go to work, pay bills, provide food, clothing and shelter for yourself and family. Moreover, having the mentality to make wise decisions as it pertains to life. I learned how to become an adult through trial and error.

Looking back at when I was 18 years of age and had my first child, I feel as a mother that at 18 years of age children have not reached a full level of maturity as of yet although society states that they have and are legal. When I gave birth to my first child I can honestly admit that I was not mentally, emotionally, or financially stable enough to rear a child. This is why sex without responsibility is dangerous and should not be taken lightly.

Although, I was a teenage mother I took the responsibility and did what I had to do to rear my child to the best of my ability with the help of my mom and granny. I never left my children with strangers or with just anyone because I did not want to be bothered with them. I laid down and had them so it was my responsibility to take care of them. I can say that I was truly blessed because although I had dropped out of school after I got pregnant; I went back to get my high school diploma a year after my child was born and went on to college for one year; college was just not for me. I even worked a full time job in the afternoon after school so I could provide for my child. My granny and my sister watched my child while I was able to get myself together so that I could be a good mom to my child. Yeah I was young and not ready; however, the choices we make in life cause you to grow up fast.

A Sistah 4 Change

To the teenagers out there who are sexually active; If you want to experience and/or have sex then by all means take caution and use preventive measures so that an unwanted pregnancy or a sexually transmitted disease will not be a factor in your life. As a parent I will not allow SOCIETY to dictate to me when my children have become mature adults. Therefore, I will continue to be an example of what a mature adult is and to teach and guide them to the best of my ability. I know they are going to make mistakes, as we all do, and even in that I hope that they learn a great lesson from them as I have from mine.

Stay at home father!
Step back to the early 20th century; during that time it was customary for the woman to stay at home and rear the children, cook, clean and take care of the family affairs while the husband went out to work as he is the provider and protector for his family.

Fast forward to the 21st century, with the employment market being as it is and people being laid off left and right increase in cost of living depending on what lifestyle you have grown accustomed to, it now takes two incomes to run a household and comfortably provide for you and your family. There are some households where both parents have to work, and then there are some where only one parent works and the other stays home and rear the children and take care of the home affairs. Well what if the parent that stays at home is the

Kimadda Agyeman

father, and the mother/wife has no problem with that. There could be a number of reasons and/or situations that caused the man to be at home.

Society says that women are to be in the home and take care of the children while the man works and brings home the check. Well the tables have turned and it seems as if the woman is making the money and can afford for the father/husband to stay home with the child/ren as well as cook and clean, and the father has no problem with that, as a matter of fact I know some couples who have come to an amicable agreement that the wife go out to work and the father stays home with the children. Everyone's home situation is different and what works for one may not work for the other. Do I view the father who stays at home as less of a man? No I do not, and although he may not be bringing home the bacon (finances) it does not mean that he cannot protect and provide for the family in other areas like emotionally, mentally and physically; these are needed as well. I have heard of some who grew up in two parent households where the father went out to work and brought home the check; however, emotionally and mentally he was not there.

Right now in my life my two children are adults and my complement and I do not have any children together, so the aforementioned does not apply to me. However, if I was in the aforementioned situation then I myself would not have any problem with going out to work and bringing the check home to provide for my family. I have been gainfully employed at the same agency for

A Sistah 4 Change

twenty-five years so even in my past relationships as well as my current I am the bread winner in the home although they were and are employed too.

I have a few scenarios why I would want my complement to stay at home. One, say that I get pregnant right? My agency only allows the mother to have 6 weeks off at the most unless, you have more leave and are financially able to stay home longer. I having a child that young, would be a bit apprehensive about putting him/her in a daycare, let alone have them to go to public school when they get school age. I would prefer for my complement if he is not gainfully employed for whatever reason be it laid off or injured and cannot work to stay at home with our child and home school. Again, this is my position and what works for some may not work for the others.

THE WOMAN THAT USES HER SISTER AS HER HAIRDRESSER, NEEDS NO MIRROR"

As black women we have always relied upon one another for upliftment, support, our image and reflection. We find the vision of ourselves in our sisters, our mothers, our grandmothers, our aunts, and our children.

Trust is an essential ingredient in all relationships. With womenfolk-our sisters-the love and caring takes on a special quality. When one has a sister friend one can share one's innermost thoughts and feelings with trust. A sister will listen to what you say, and tell you what you need to hear.

Kimadda Agyeman

You will want for your sister what you want for yourself. She will readily give to you what she would have for herself. Therefore, there is no need for mirrors between sisters. You will see yourself in her eyes as she does in yours. The image is of beauty, caring and noble composure.

As the bearers and nurturers of the race/nation black women must ascend to our rightful place – a place where and when there is no longer a need for mirrors between us.

-Nsenga Warfield-Coppock

Thought Topic Chapter 10
The Beauty of Sistahood

A sister can be seen as someone who is both ourselves and very much not ourselves – a special kind of double.
Toni Morrison

I love my sisters to pieces and there is nothing that I would not do for them if it is in my power to do and within reason. I am speaking of my sisters in my family who I grew up with in the same home as well as the sisters that are in my extended family. I value sistahood and I want what is best for my sisters. It was October 2008 and I was going through a transition in my life mentally, physically and spiritually. While on social media I would post a lot of inspirational posts and graphics. I would impart words of wisdom to enlighten those on my friends list; coupled with that because of who I am which is a cool down to earth sistah whose

Kimadda Agyeman

spirit is very inviting and approachable a lot of the sisters felt compelled to reach out to me.

During that time I was speaking with a lot of these sisters on social media; most of them would just pour their hearts out. I mean these sisters did not know me outside of social media; however, for some reason or another they felt comfortable sharing their most personal and intimate thoughts with me. Most of the times I just listened and let them speak because sometimes you don't always have to say anything. Then there were times where I was compelled to speak and share and give them some wisdom and insight into what they were dealing with at that time. Moreover, the brothers who were on my friends list would reach out to me in hopes that I could give them advice on their relationship with their complement, because they noticed some areas in their woman's life that maybe another sistah of a certain caliber could help out with. I tell you I was just elated that these sisters and brothers sought me out amongst all those other sisters who were doing the same thing I was doing or something similar.

While on a week off from work I decided to go on a fast. During that time I ate no food, watched no television, no radio or use the computer. I just shut everything down and went within myself as I do from time to time; I like to do a lot of introspection and reflect on a lot that has transpired in my life. As I went within myself I kept a journal and pen beside me to write and express what I was feeling. By the end of the week the vision and the mission of Sistaz 4 Ma'at formerly

A Sistah 4 Change

known as Sistaz 4 Change was birthed.

In hind sight I realized that all the time these sisters and brothers were reaching out to me for guidance and wisdom I was being prepared to launch my sistahood community/organization to create a safe haven where sisters can come and share and strengthen one another as we all have traveled many roads and for some reason we all seem to end up on the same path leading to the door of redemption and wholeness.

One thing I must admit about forming a sistahood community is that some, not all of the times, we sisters have so many issues with one another. There is jealousy, envy, competition and all sorts of other character traits that can damage a sistahood. I try my best to work and reach out and unite with my sisters by all means necessary as I know and understand the importance of having a sister who you can relate too and become vulnerable with. It really saddens me when we sisters treat one another bad or do things to hurt another sister for whatever reason.

There is one sister in particular, although I have met many who I like to give mention of, Victoria. This sister and I never met in person, we met online in 2009. She lives out of state, so we built our relationship by phone and over the internet. When I met this sister instantly I knew that we had traveled the same paths in life and we meshed. I think of the times when we would be on the phone just crying and sharing in one another's pain and even in the joy's that transpired in our lives. I could be vulnerable to this sister and share my deepest innermost feelings and she could with me and I never once felt judged by her or her by me. There were times that months would go by and I did not hear from her and although I know that she is a woman of strength; I could sense in my spirit when something was not right. The times that we did speak after that it felt like we had just spoken the day before.

It is 2013 and I still have not met this sister in person due to our schedules. However, I know when the time comes and we do meet in the flesh it will be a joy to my heart. Just as much as she has learned from me. I have learned from her; because of who she is there is no need for a mirror.

In closing as I have written throughout this book that I have experienced much in my life, and I made a vow that I would work diligently to change the negative circumstances that had transpired in my life. Once that healing and restoration took place and was evident I said that I would go and assist my sisters with whatever they were dealing with and help with restoring healing and balance to their lives. I share the poem on the preceding page as a testament to what my foundation was established to do. A sisters mission is to unite with others to form a bond of sistahood. I am my sisters keeper.

Closing Thoughts

"A wise person will always find a way"
Tanzanian proverb

As an Afrikan Centered woman who has gained knowledge of self I write not only to appease those who are in the "conscious community" I write to the spirit and soul of the Black woman, man and child here in the Diaspora and on the continent.

Although, the topics in this book speak to the current mental state and condition of my Black sisters and brothers as these are the issues that plague us in the community in which I live; the Afrikan proverbs and wisdom presented in this book cross all nationalities and cultures and if they are embraced with an open mind, they can be of a benefit to anyone who has experienced and/or experiencing some of the same things that I have experienced in my life.

We as Afrikans live in a world that is forever changing and depending where you are, at this juncture in your life, either you are on the side of those who embrace change or the side of those who fear and reject change. I embrace change and personally feel that change is a good thing.

As you have taken this journey with me you have glimpsed into the events that have transpired in my life and the various stages and levels of knowledge and wisdom I acquired and maturity in how I handled those events. In order for me to reach this plateau I had to embrace change because If I did not I would have become stagnated and remained in a state or condition which would have been detrimental to my life and well-being.

Finally, we are evolving as a people whether those of you care to see that or not; and during this process we are forever in a perpetual state of learning and growing. I say don't become stagnate as you may just miss out on what this vast universe has in store for you.

Peace, Love & Light

Appendix A
Glossary of Terms

Ankh

The ankh also known as key of life, the key of the Nile or crux ansata (Latin meaning "cross with a handle"), was the ancient Egyptian hieroglyphic character that read "life", a triliteral sign for the consonants. It represents the concept of eternal life, which is the general meaning of the symbol. The Egyptian gods are often portrayed carrying it by its loop, or bearing one in each hand, arms crossed over their chest

Consciousness

The quality or state of being aware of an external object or something within oneself. It has been defined as: subjectivity, awareness, sentience, the ability to experience or to feel, wakefulness, having a sense of self hood, and the executive control system of the mind.

Kimadda Agyeman

Maafa

African Holocaust, Holocaust of Enslavement, or Black holocaust as alternativesare terms used to describe the history and on-going effects of atrocities inflicted on African people. The Maafa is held to have started with the Arab and Atlantic slave trades, and continued through imperialism, colonialism, and other forms of oppression to the present day.

Mentacide

The planned and systematic destruction of a group's mentality aimed at the destruction of the group." Thus, Black folk alienated from their culture and history eventually lose their sense of purpose and direction, the symptoms of Mentacide. - Bobby E Wright

Pan Afrikan -RBG

Pan-Africanism is an ideology and movement that encourages the solidarity of Africans worldwide.[1] It is based on the belief that unity is vital to economic, social, and political progress and aims to "unify and uplift" people of African descent. The ideology asserts that the fates of all African peoples and countries are intertwined. At its core Pan-Africanism is "a belief that African peoples, both on the continent and in the Diaspora, share not merely a common history, but a common destiny"

Re-Afrikinization:

Historians refer to this process as 're-Africanization,' meaning the "intentional assertion of aesthetics, theologies, and practices considered more African.

A Sistah 4 Change

Sankofa

Sankofa can mean either the word in the Akan language of Ghana that translates in English to "go back and get it or the Asante Adinkra symbols of a bird with its head turned backwards taking an egg off its back, or of a stylised heart shape. It is often associated with the proverb, "Se wo were fi na wosankofa a yenkyi," which translates "It is not wrong to go back for that which you have forgotten."

Appendix B
Author's Contact

I would love to hear from you and to read your thoughts and perspectives on these topics as well as answer any other questions you may have. You can reach me at the contact below.

Kimadda Agyeman Enterprise
P.O. Box 91837
Washington D.C. 20090
www.kimaddaagyeman.com
info@kimaddaagyeman.com

www.ingramcontent.com/pod-product-compliance
Lightning Source LLC
LaVergne TN
LVHW091207080426
835509LV00006B/875